Barbara Walters **Jane Pauley** **Connie Chung**

WOMEN WHO BROKE BARRIERS
The New Face of TV News

Charlayne Hunter-Gault **Theresa Gutierrez** **Christiane Amanpour**

By Lou Ann Walker

CELEBRATION PRESS
Pearson Learning Group

CONTENTS

THEN AND NOW

A 1950s family watches a TV news program.

Imagine you click your television's remote control, and on the screen, you see the evening news. A woman reporter may be standing in front of the White House, telling about a president's speech. There's nothing unusual about this scene, right?

Actually, if television watchers from the 1950s saw this broadcast, they would most likely be astonished. When the television industry first started and during the next several decades, women were rarely seen onscreen delivering or reporting the news. Minorities represented an even smaller fraction of women in broadcasting.

Milestones for Women

1948 The first nightly newscast debuts on CBS.

1963 CBS expands evening newscasts from 15 to 30 minutes long.

1945   1950   1955   1960   1965   1970

1952 The *Today* show premieres on NBC—the first morning news and entertainment program.

Barbara Walters **1974** becomes the first woman co-host of *Today*.

What happened to change the face of broadcast news? At the time, women faced the same barriers in almost all professions. There were very few women doctors, lawyers, bankers, or college presidents. As the women's movement and equality for racial minorities took hold, television, radio, magazines, and newspapers all reported on the developments. It wasn't long before those sources realized that they could not be **hypocrites**. If broadcast news was **advocating** for better roles for women and minorities, then those same outlets would have to start hiring women and minorities.

A few pioneering women began training for jobs

in TV News

1976 Barbara Walters, the first woman to co-host the evening news, joins Harry Reasoner on ABC.

1995 Connie Chung leaves the network evening news.

75   1980   1985   1990

1993 Connie Chung joins *CBS Evening News with Dan Rather*, the second female co-anchor in television history.

in broadcasting. However, being a pioneer entailed many hardships. Men were reluctant to give up powerful, high-paying, high-profile jobs. Women argued that they had to work much harder than men did to get promotions.

Women also had to work against various kinds of **discrimination**. They had to conquer the perception that they were less serious. Some of them gave up the idea of marriage and a family and devoted themselves to their jobs in order to prove they could do the work. Others were discriminated against because they were too young or too old, or because of their ethnic backgrounds. As a result, the women who succeeded in the broadcast news business had to be tough, **tenacious**, and clever. On the air, they had to demonstrate grace under pressure.

Today, women make up nearly 40 percent of the staff in television newsrooms. The morning programs, such as *Today* and *Good Morning America*, which combine news and entertainment, have been especially important as a way for women to prove their talents on the air. For example, Barbara Walters and Jane Pauley both got their first national recognition on *Today*. One of their successors, Katie Couric, is the highest paid woman in all of TV news, earning about $15 million per year in 2002.

Certainly, not all women in TV news today have great jobs and fat paychecks. Yet the excitement of being where the action is and knowing what's going on in the world keeps many women in broadcasting.

In this book, you'll read profiles of six women in television broadcast news who have worked their way to the top of their profession. Every one of them started at the bottom in a low-paying job. Every one of them faced unkind comments. Every one worked extremely long hours to get to the top and stay there. Every one broke a barrier against women in the TV industry. For them, the rewards—power and respect, the satisfaction of meeting extreme challenges—have made the hardships worthwhile.

BARBARA WALTERS

Pioneer Continues to Make News

In the mid-1970s, Barbara Walters was the first female co-host of NBC's *Today* show.

Seemingly, Barbara Walters had an easy life as a child in New York City. Her father, a famous nightclub owner and theatrical producer, led a glamorous life. She was introduced to many celebrities, and she went to the best schools.

The reality was very different. By the time her glamorous father died, he had no money. As Walters was growing up, her father had meant to teach her not to worry about anything. Based on what happened, Walters had the opposite reaction. "The lesson I learned *was* to worry," she says.

The truth behind Walters' rise in the news business is not so surprising. She got to the pinnacle, the top of the business, through persistence, hard work, and being greatly liked by others.

In the 1960s, when Walters got her first real job as a writer for *Today*, the program had a limit of one woman writer. Another woman could get that job only if the woman writer quit. Walters really wanted the job of co-host of the show. She wasn't considered attractive enough to be on camera, but she **persevered** with executives until she got the job in 1974.

Two years later, television industry insiders considered her too "inexperienced" to be a network evening news **co-anchor**. Yet, on April 20, 1976,

In 1976, Barbara Walters became a co-anchor of ABC News with Harry Reasoner.

she made television history by becoming the first ever woman to co-anchor for a network evening news program. Her contract with ABC was for a startling $1 million, which included her work on separate prime-time interview shows, talking with international newsmakers and celebrities.

Still, Walters more than earned her salary. The next year, the heads of state of two warring countries, Egypt and Israel, appeared on her show together. The two men had been long-time foes.

People found all kinds of reasons to criticize Barbara Walters. In her early years, people knocked her simply because she was female. The press and comedians made fun of her inability to pronounce *r*'s. Once she walked into her daughter's room while a comedian on television was making fun of her. Walters was embarrassed in front of her daughter, but then her daughter said, "Oh, Mother! Lighten up!" "And I did," Walters says. "I thought, what am I so serious about? In a funny way, it's a compliment."

Other people joked about her choice of questions. For instance, she has been known to ask movie stars if they were a tree, what kind would they be. Though some of her questions have seemed lightweight, Walters nearly always wins over her subjects. Many famous people are eager to be interviewed by her, and they enjoy the discussions.

Despite the publicity of being the first to have a woman co-anchor, the ABC evening newscast suffered in the ratings. In 1978, the network switched the format and began using several anchors. Walters was not troubled by the setbacks or the criticism. She began working harder than ever on her *Barbara Walters Specials*. She scored high ratings every year, particularly with her programs that aired right before the Academy Awards programs. Over the years, she has interviewed nearly every big name in Hollywood.

For many years, Walters has been the co-host of *20/20*, another frequently top-rated evening program of news and features. She is also the co-founder, co-executive producer, and a star of the daytime show *The View*. She appears along with four other women who work together as co-hosts.

Looking back on her long career, Walters says, "I had the opportunity to do the most important thing, and that was prove myself to myself. It has been, for me, a career beyond my dreams." She does have one regret, however. She never kept a diary of the people she has met and the incredible events she has attended in her extraordinary life.

JANE PAULEY
Balancing Celebrity and Family Privacy

The NBC *Today* show cast in 1982, left to right: Chris Wallace, Gene Shalit, Jane Pauley, Willard Scott, and Bryant Gumbel.

Jane Pauley was born and grew up in Indiana. In high school, she was on the speech and debate team. This was excellent training for a woman who would go on to become a television legend.

Nevertheless, she might not have gotten her first interview had the Federal Communications Commission not had a requirement that television stations hire female reporters. The news director of Indianapolis's WISH-TV was also reluctant to interview someone right out of college. "The minute I saw her on camera, I knew she was something special," he said.

Starting as a cub, or new, reporter, Pauley was soon working regularly in front of the camera. Her writing was so good that experienced writers at the station came to her for help with their stories.

She soon moved to Chicago's WMAQ-TV where, in 1975, she became the first woman to ever co-anchor that city's weeknight news program. Within a year, she had been selected from 2,000 other people for Barbara Walters' job at *Today*. Critics complained that Pauley was too young, too pretty, and too cheery for the job. Nevertheless, *Today* soon became number one in the morning ratings. At its height, millions of people tuned in to NBC every morning.

The work was constantly exciting. Pauley covered the royal wedding of Prince Charles and Lady Diana Spencer in London. She visited the Great Wall of China. She also anchored the Sunday evening news for NBC from 1980 to 1982.

In 1980, Pauley married syndicated *Doonesbury* cartoonist, Garry Trudeau. They became parents of twins, Ross and Rachel, and later had another son, Thomas. Pauley's first priority has been to protect her children from the glare of public life. "[When I go home, I leave] my celebrity at the door," she said. She talks openly about herself but never permits her children to be interviewed or photographed. Indeed, when Rachel was 12, she asked her mother for advice about becoming a TV journalist. Pauley said, "If [she] takes my advice—and it will be given, not imposed—she'll get a liberal arts education. She probably won't major in journalism; maybe she'll minor in it. I would encourage her to major in something else: history, English, economics, a foreign language."

She has always upheld the highest **ethics** of journalism. "I am absolutely wedded to the idea of objectivity and fairness," Pauley says. She has received several journalism and broadcast awards and works with groups to improve education in broadcast journalism.

Pauley is also well known for being considerate of others. In 1989, after 13 years, *Today* planned to replace Pauley with a younger woman named Deborah Norville. Viewers and critics alike expected fireworks. They were stunned at how graciously and sincerely Pauley welcomed Norville to the show and said goodbye. "It was the first major bump in my career, and I had to deal with it," she said. "I . . . recognized a confidence and strength that were unfamiliar to me, and I like them."

Over the years, Pauley has hosted several documentaries, including *Women, Work and Babies*, as well as MSNBC's *Time & Again*. In 1992, she became co-host on *Dateline NBC*, a three-night-per-week newsmagazine that has won many awards and top ratings. "She doesn't do the investigative, breaking news stories," her *Dateline* boss said. "What Jane does best are the stories where she can really connect with people, real triumph over tragedy." In 1998, the show added a fourth night, making Jane Pauley the first woman in television history to co-host four hours of weekly prime-time news programming. By 1998, Pauley's yearly salary was about $5.5 million.

Pauley admits she's competitive. "You want to be king of the hill," she says. However, in 2001, she stunned network executives by taking a long leave of absence, returning to *Dateline* in the fall. She had needed time to recover from an illness, a form of hives

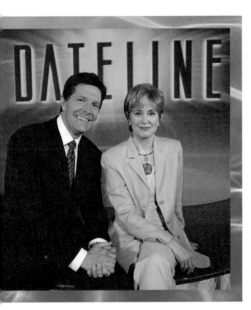

Stone Phillips and Jane Pauley, co-hosts of *Dateline NBC*, celebrate the show's tenth year in 2002.

that had caused her face to swell. She had also worked on her memoirs and spent time with her children before they went to college, showing that her family and personal life were still her first **priorities**.

CONNIE CHUNG

Daughter of Immigrants

Connie Chung conducts an interview at the Republican Convention in 1984.

Constance Yu-Hwa Chung, whose name means "Princess Ivory," was the last of her parents' ten children and the only one born in the United States, their adopted homeland. They had left China after losing five children to the country's high infant mortality.

Sons are revered in traditional Chinese culture, and Connie felt her father's disappointment that she wasn't a boy. She partly credits her aggressive drive for success in the news business to the desire to make it up to her father for being born female.

As a little girl living in Washington, D.C., Chung used to grab the vacuum cleaner hose and pretend to do news interviews. Although she was always interested in politics, she began college as a biology major. However, she soon switched to what she loved best: journalism.

After graduation, Chung began her television career in 1969 with her first job at WTTG-TV in Washington, D.C., as a newsroom secretary—about the only job open to women in TV in those days. By 1970, the push to hire women and minorities at television stations gave Chung the chance to work as a writer, then as a reporter. In 1971, she became a *CBS News* national correspondent and covered the 1972 presidential race. "She was small and pretty," one co-worker said, "but she could elbow with the best of them. She was not some flower one could push aside."

Always on the move, Chung became anchor of a news program in Los Angeles at a local station in 1976. By 1983, she returned east and accepted a job at NBC, which included anchoring Saturday evening news reports, *NBC News at Sunrise*, and many specials.

Rejoining CBS in 1989, she was given a variety of top assignments, including news magazine programs called *Saturday Night with Connie Chung* and *Eye to Eye with Connie Chung*. Then, in 1993, she was paired with veteran anchor Dan Rather and became the second woman, after Barbara Walters, to co-anchor a

Connie Chung broadcasts the news on CBS in 1992.

weeknight evening news program.

Chung has covered many elections and has managed to be the only reporter to interview people at the center of some important news stories. For example, Connie Chung held the only TV interview with the captain of the ship *Exxon-Valdez* after it caused the Alaskan oil spill.

Her reporting and interviewing has brought her three Emmy awards. In 1999–2000, she won a human rights award for her story about abused young women in Bangladesh. Another of her investigations led to a murder indictment of a man who had been freed 33 years earlier due to a lack of evidence. In 2002, she joined the cable news channel

CNN and began traveling around the world to cover breaking stories.

According to entertainment writers, Chung has always combined solid **professionalism** and smooth delivery with a natural, relaxed charm. Her "Q-ratings," measurements of the popularity of people on television, have been extremely high. In 2002, she became host of the prime-time CNN program *Connie Chung Tonight*. The highly advertised program has news stories and interviews, both of which display many of Chung's strengths. On the program's first night, about 850,000 people watched.

Chung's work often has seemed to come before her personal life. However, she met Maury Povich, a fellow journalist and daytime talk show host, early in her career. In 1977, they were matched as news anchors on a Los Angeles program. They fell in love and later married. In 1995, the couple adopted a son, Matthew. Chung still worries about balancing motherhood and a career. "It is virtually impossible to feel that I am doing a good job at both ends," she says.

Chung is proud of her more than 30 years of experience in the news business. Moving to CNN was a gamble, some critics believed, but she looked forward to the challenge. "I believe CNN is the last sanctuary for just news," Chung said.

CHARLAYNE HUNTER-GAULT

Newsmaker to News Reporter

Charlayne Hunter (center) is escorted to classes at the
University of Georgia on January 12, 1961.

Long before she was a news reporter, Charlayne
Hunter-Gault was a major newsmaker. In 1961, she
was one of two African Americans to integrate the
University of Georgia. They entered the school as
white students shouted protests.

Charlayne Hunter was born in Due West, South
Carolina, the first of three children. Her mother,
Althea, had hoped for a boy so that he could be
named "Charles Junior," after his father. When a girl
was born, her mother simply created a female
version of the name.

Hunter-Gault's father, a U.S. Army chaplain, was posted in many places around the world. In some places, Hunter-Gault faced much discrimination. At dances in Alaska at which she was the only African American girl, no one asked her to dance except for a teacher. She was also denied admission to a club for teens. When her parents divorced and she moved with her mother and two brothers to Atlanta, Georgia, she found that African Americans were refused service in restaurants. She did not let these incidents bother her and applied herself to her schoolwork. When she thought about college, she realized she wanted to study journalism.

African American leaders wanted to **desegregate** Georgia universities and asked Hunter-Gault and a young man named Hamilton Holmes to apply to the University of Georgia. They were admitted, but the college put many roadblocks in their paths. So, Hunter-Gault began her studies in Michigan. She transferred to Georgia after several court rulings against the university. The second night she was in her dorm, a brick and a bottle were thrown through her window. The state troopers removed her from the school. She was readmitted after two more trips to court. Students pounded on the floor above to keep her awake at night. Her car was scratched and her tires flattened. "Their rocks, their bricks, their spit never touched me," Hunter-Gault said, "because in my head I was an African queen."

She continued breaking barriers outside of school, too. She had a summer **internship** at the Louisville, Kentucky, *Times* newspaper, then earned a position at the **prestigious** *New Yorker* magazine after she graduated from the University of Georgia. She was the first African American on staff at these periodicals.

Hunter-Gault enjoyed working at the *New Yorker*, yet she wanted to prove herself in the rough-and-tumble world of journalism. "It was very important to me to establish myself as a journalist," she says. "I had been famous at nineteen for something that should ordinarily have required no effort other than . . . getting good grades. . . . I was famous because I had walked onto the campus of the University of Georgia. I was famous for being black. . . . But I wanted to be famous for something that I could do, that rested really on my abilities."

She went to Washington's WRC-TV as an investigative reporter and anchorwoman. In 1968, Hunter-Gault moved to *The New York Times*, eventually becoming the Harlem bureau chief. She won three Publishers Awards for her outstanding stories.

Her career in broadcast news began in 1978 when she joined the *MacNeil/Lehrer Report* on PBS, becoming one of the first African American female television correspondents. During her 19 years on the program, Hunter-Gault's work was highly regarded. She covered the Middle East, Africa, and the Caribbean. During the MacNeil-Lehrer years, she won two Emmy awards, as well as a Peabody Award for a series called *Apartheid's People.*

In 1992, Hunter-Gault published her book, *In My Place*, in which she talked about the discrimination she faced. "We have to make room for all of the voices," Hunter-Gault said. "I don't think you get at universal truth with one set of eyes. You need many."

Charlayne Hunter-Gault worked as a news correspondent at PBS when she published her book, *In My Place.*

In 1997 she moved with her husband, financial expert, Ron Gault, to South Africa and became a reporter for National Public Radio (NPR). She reported on the end of apartheid. She calls South Africa "one of the greatest challenges that we in the media face."

THERESA GUTIERREZ
Opening Doors for Latinas

Theresa Gutierrez (second from right) conducts an interview for ABC7 in Chicago in 1985.

When Theresa Gutierrez (pronounced *goo-tair-ez*) began knocking on doors in Chicago in the early 1970s to get a job in broadcasting, she didn't have much success. She grew up outside of Gary, Indiana, dreaming of living in a big city. She loved acting, had appeared in many summer productions, and had taken television courses during her college years at Indiana University. Yet, breaking into television was scary. "At that time women didn't have important roles in the media," Gutierrez said. Still, she added, "I didn't accept the nos."

Finally, Gutierrez was chosen for a paid internship at NBC in Chicago. When the internship was over, she applied for a job as a production assistant and was chosen over 200 other applicants. She proved herself by working 12 to 14 hours a day. "I have that work ethic from my parents."

In 1973, Gutierrez started the additional job of moderator on a women's show on WLS radio. In four months, she was also doing a show on Latino social and economic issues in Chicago. "I really didn't want to do Latino issues. I didn't want to be pigeonholed. If I didn't do it, no one would," she said.

After breaking down doors to get into television journalism, Gutierrez faced the next hurdle: to go from doing specialized shows to being a news reporter. "Being Latina was very difficult. Everyone else was blond haired and blue eyed. It was a tough fight to get into news," she said. The general manager of her station told her that she should go to the Southwest, where her look would fit in. "Why don't we go to Michigan Avenue and see if people think I'm offensive?" Gutierrez demanded.

"When you're one of the first, there is a lot of you that's chipped away," Gutierrez said. "The fight to open doors for other Latinas is very important to me. You can *never* give up. You can never crumble."

Gutierrez kept on fighting. "I was constantly nagging

the executives, sending them memos," she said. The executives kept saying no because they didn't think the Latino community was important.

She is convinced that the real reason the station finally gave her a chance in 1986 was because of her outside work with community groups. "My parents taught me you have to give back. You can't just take," Gutierrez said. Evenings and weekends she worked for various social causes. She says she also gained a great deal while doing it. Different people from the charities

Theresa Gutierrez hosted a show on ABC7 called "Feminine Franchise" in 1972.

and community groups began calling the station and asking why Gutierrez wasn't on the air more.

After becoming an on-air reporter, Gutierrez acknowledges how tough the work is. "The air part is very simple. Gathering news is hard. A minute thirty takes pounding on doors, hanging out at police stations." In every story she tries to find something she's passionate about, but she admits the news business places a constant struggle on everyone. "You never pay your dues," Gutierrez adds. "You're only as good as your last story."

Her advice to young people? "Prepare yourself, balance your life, and set priorities and goals."

How Theresa Gutierrez Has Triumphed

- One of the first Latino women to break into broadcasting in the United States
- General assignment reporter for Chicago's ABC7 News since 1986
- Winner, the Triunfo Achievement Award from the Latino Coalition on the Media
- In 1999, included as one of 100 women "Making a Difference" by *Chicago Woman Magazine*
- Named one of six outstanding broadcasters in the United States by *Hispanic USA Magazine*

- Involved in community service organizations, including Chicago Sister Cities International Program, Access Living, On Our Own Hear Our Cries (for victims of domestic violence)
- Works with Kids International Surgical Services (K.I.S.S.), which, in 1999, raised money to bring Baby Santiago from Mexico for brain surgery
- Host of Chicago's Puerto Rican and Mexican Independence parades
- Host of *Tapestry*, a TV program on Latinos making positive contributions

CHRISTIANE AMANPOUR
War Reporter

Christiane Amanpour broadcasts news on wars and conflicts around the world.

In 1983, Christiane Amanpour arrived at CNN's Atlanta bureau with a suitcase, a bicycle, and about $100, looking for a job at the new cable news network. She had a journalism degree and had worked as an intern at a small television station. She was tired of hearing that her long name, British accent, and different looks were problems. Finally, her determination paid off. At CNN she was hired as an assistant on the foreign desk. "She said she wanted to be a star," one of her bosses said. "We all smiled."

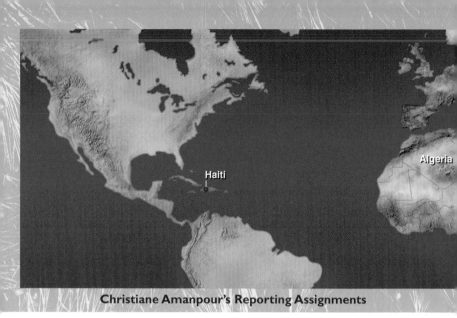

Christiane Amanpour's Reporting Assignments

Amanpour was used to challenges. The daughter of an Iranian father and a British mother, she was living with her family in Tehran, Iran, in 1979 when the Iranian revolution erupted. Her family lost everything. Amanpour, 20, went to England, then on to the United States. Her grandmother paid her tuition so that she could study journalism at the University of Rhode Island.

At CNN, Amanpour worked her way up from lowly **gofer** to writer, producer, field producer, and finally, to reporter. Today, she's one of the few female war correspondents in the world. When she reports for CNN, millions of viewers in many countries watch her. She also works as a contributor to CBS's *60 Minutes*.

She has been in Iraq, East Timor, Chechnya, Afghanistan, and Israel's West Bank during the most violent times in recent history. Her stories from Bosnia made her world famous.

Amanpour, who has turned down anchor positions that would take her away from the front, admits she is fascinated by the "intensity" of war reporting. "It's pure adrenalin," she has said.

On assignment, she lives for long periods of time without running water or electricity. Her life is often in peril. A co-worker said, "Christiane's like a cat. She's got the best instincts for knowing when to get in and out." One of her CNN bosses declared,

"Christiane's fearless." He added that he worries "because she thinks bullets bounce off her." That may be how she appears to others; however, Amanpour wears a helmet and flak vest when she's at the battle front. She figured out that she has spent more time on the battlefield than most soldiers.

Seeing horrific events has been hard. She admits she spends her working life "scared of being shot, of being kidnapped." Many of her friends have been killed. Her camera operator needed plastic surgery after she was hit in the face by a Serbian sniper's bullet. Indeed, she calls war reporting "something that gives you a chance to confront your fears." One night she heard "an awful whistling noise." A howitzer shell landed two rooms down from hers in her Sarajevo hotel, but by some miracle, didn't explode.

On her reporting beat, she met State Department spokesman James Rubin. They married in 1998 and have a son, Darius. But because of her hectic reporting schedule, she's often away from her family. "We talk an enormous amount on the phone," her husband said, "and we see each other on TV." Her short days are 12 hours long. The others? "Around the clock." Amanpour's list of awards is long, including a Courage in Journalism Award, a Golden Cable ACE for her Gulf War coverage, two Peabody Awards, and two George Polk Awards.

Ironically, Amanpour has said that, "Writing stories, not dodging bullets, is the hardest part of my work."

What she likes most about her job is focusing people's attention on important world events. What's crucial is "being there and bearing witness," she said.

When asked why she continues to report from war fronts, she replies, "If we . . . don't . . ., then the bad people will win. I believe that good journalism, good television, can make our world a better place."

What's the next barrier to be broken by women like Christiane Amanpour? The list of

In 2000, Christiane Amanpour reported on conflicts in Jerusalem.

women who dream of a network news solo anchor slot is long. The number of girls and young women studying, working hard, and preparing themselves for that possibility is large, too.

GLOSSARY

advocating	publicly urging or supporting a cause
co-anchor	a person who shares the major hosting duties on a news program; anchors read the news and introduce segments from reporters in the field
desegregate	integrate, or bring together, people of different races in public institutions such as schools
discrimination	showing prejudice against a person or people based on their race, gender, or age
ethics	dealing with right and wrong of actions
gofer	slang for someone who runs errands
hypocrites	people who say one thing, but believe the opposite
internship	a temporary job in which a young person gains supervised, practical experience in an area
persevered	persisted in doing something, despite difficulties or obstacles
prestigious	having a high reputation
priorities	ranking choices in order of importance
professionalism	behaving in a way that reflects well on a person's position
tenacious	keeping a firm hold; persistent